I Didn't Sign Up for This . . .

One Dementia Caregiver's Personal
Story and How She Survived

MARY MONROE

authorHOUSE®

AuthorHouse™
1663 Liberty Drive
Bloomington, IN 47403
www.authorhouse.com
Phone: 1 (800) 839-8640

Published by AuthorHouse 02/25/2019

ISBN: 978-1-5462-7949-5 (sc)
ISBN: 978-1-5462-7948-8 (e)

Library of Congress Control Number: 2019901384

Print information available on the last page.

*This book is dedicated to my husband, Mike Monroe,
who exemplifies courage and strength.*

*It is also dedicated to the
over 40 million family caregivers
who selflessly care for their loved ones.*

*Rules for Happiness:
Something to do, someone to love, something to hope for.
—Immanuel Kant*

Contents

Chapter 1

The Day Your Life Changes Forever

Perhaps you saw the early signs of dementia in your loved one but refused to acknowledge them. Or, you were sharply acute and noticed the definite cognitive changes in your loved one immediately – it doesn't matter. What matters is that your life changed forever the day you realized that your spouse or loved one had dementia and your world would never be the same again.

For me, it was a time of mourning, a time of death – death of our future plans, death of our "golden years," and death to our various relationships throughout 40 years – first as boyfriend and girlfriend, then lovers, and then as marriage partners. Without memories, how could these various relationships still exist? Without conversation, how could they be real?

"I didn't sign up for this," I lamented to myself. I had imagined Mike and I growing old together, enjoying the fruits of our labors of employment over decades, saving for and paying off our family home. I had imagined wonderful, shared moments spent with our grown children and grandchildren. It shocked my mind. What happened? It wasn't supposed to turn out this way!

You might say, "Well, you did sign up for it when you married your husband on Oct. 22, 1977, and repeated those vows, '. . . in sickness and in health.'" And in my heart, I knew that was true. I would never desert my husband in his time of need, but it didn't mean I would have to be happy about this horrible disease robbing us of our dreams. But in my usual manner of dealing with life's inevitable ups and downs, I tackled this project with all the gusto I had. This book is my personal story of how I survived as a dementia caregiver, and I am writing it to provide some words of advice, tips, and lessons-learned to other people who find themselves in this exclusive "club" as dementia caregivers. It was a six-year journey that I wouldn't wish on my worst enemy, but by the grace of God, I survived and even thrived to be where I am today. You can, and will, too.

I remember one time when Mike (my husband, Mike Monroe of Westmont, IL. and then Lake Worth, FL., now deceased as of 7/22/18) was in the early diagnosis of dementia and he was sitting in an easy chair in our living room, looking totally normal. But it was at this moment that I realized that our lives would be changed forever, and I was filled with a deep sense of loss. I'm not a big "crier," but I could see everything that we had hoped for in our future simply slipping away, and I was filled with a deep sorrow and tears flooded my eyes. I said to him, "Honey, I'm so sorry we're going to have to go through this. It's not fair and we didn't deserve it. I can't say goodbye to everything we have built together. I don't want to say goodbye to us," and he just looked at me, blankly, as if he didn't realize or understand the ramifications of what he was going to be going through. Either he was dealing with it privately, or this hideous disease gives the sufferer one blessing – to not understand fully what exactly the future holds for them, and how this disease will eventually reduce them to a hollow shell of their true inner person. How this disease will turn their life upside down, inside out, and take them on a rocky journey with little or no control over situations or outcomes. How this disease leaves a caregiver spent, empty, angry, sad, forlorn, and wondering when or how she can ever go back to living life fully again.

Let me take you back to the day I met Mike. It was the 4th of July weekend of the summer of 1976, and the entire country was celebrating the Bicentennial 200 Year Anniversary of our country. We had both graduated from college by then – Mike from Southern Illinois University and me from Northern Illinois University. The 70's were the best years to be alive as a young adult — people believed in peace, love, and good times. Raggedy cut offs, skimpy bikinis, and crop tops were the outfits of the day. I was living in Chicago at the time, working at an ad agency as a copywriter. Two of my close friends had graduated from SIU and were mutual friends of Mike, who was having a big 4th of July weekend-long party with his large group of friends. We piled into an old VW bug and headed the 7 hours south to SIU, making jokes about meeting our future husbands, playfully speaking in girlish voices with Southern accents.

When I met Mike, I guess you could say it was love at first sight. Mike and I were sitting next to each other that night on the stairs of an old college rental home watching the fireworks. When he put his arm around me while fireworks were literally going off all around us at the same time, I felt so comfortable, like this is where I'm supposed to be, and this is who I'm supposed to be with.

On Oct. 22, 1977, Mike and I were married, and we moved to Lake Worth, Florida, in 1979 after one of Chicago's worst winters, the Blizzard of '79. As young newlyweds, we shared so many experiences, from temporarily living in the "Tip Top Hotel" in Florida for weeks until we purchased our first home, eating one of our first homemade dinners of a simple roasted chicken on makeshift chairs and a round wooden crate table, and driving to Louisville, Kentucky, in a pick-up truck while I was pregnant with our first child, Michelle, to see Mike's favorite sport event of all time – The Kentucky Derby. As we became young parents, our bonds grew, from tackling the usual parenting dilemmas like night-time feedings, children with chicken pox, and never seeming to have enough time to do it all. We didn't go out much – we were living on very modest salaries – so our family times were spent with home-cooked meals, church events and trips back home. As our family grew to include a boy, Mark, and two more daughters, Marcie and Melody, we moved to an acre of land in our same community and had our "Monroe family home" built to our specifications. We were known as the "M & M family" and we were living the "American Dream," and our children were all involved with school and sports activities such as horseback riding, hockey, softball, baseball, basketball and volleyball. We had many, many wonderful friends and neighbors with whom we shared many celebrations and parties, including our signature, legacy event – our huge, annual New Year's Eve parties.

Those moments of a long-term marriage are like the woven threads of a tapestry; they create a bond so strong that we felt nothing could come between us. Our marriage wasn't perfect; it was filled with ups and downs of various trials and tribulations. Nothing tested the strength of our marriage more than when we lost our firstborn daughter in 2004 in a tragic car accident; she was just 22. Many marriages break up after a loss as deep as this; however, we vowed to each other and to our children to remain strong as a family as a legacy to Michelle, because that is what she would have wanted.

I never thought anything else could come into our lives with the impact of that loss, and I had looked forward to a long marriage with Mike. Both of our parents had celebrated long marriages – over 50 years. I had told my children many times that dad and I would take them on a wonderful trip to celebrate our 40th anniversary as it was just a few years away — with all expenses paid! So, it seemed quite surreal that on Oct. 22, 2017, my 40th anniversary, I found myself alone in my home. Mike had just been placed in an assisted living facility because we could no longer care for him at home. My two daughters and I took him out of his new home of just a few weeks to a local Tex-Mex restaurant. Mike faced many difficulties during this little celebration from forgetting how to get into the car, how to sit in a booth, and even hold his burger. He was showing signs of visual hallucinations as he was reaching down on the floor to pick up imaginary items and trying to eat scraps of food off the ground.

I am sharing my story with you because I did survive. It was a very hard six-year journey as a caregiver to my husband of 40 years, and now becoming a widow. But, if I can do it, you can and will too. Yes, I'm still standing and putting one foot in front of the other every day, and I owe it to a deep faith in a higher power, a positive attitude and a never-give-up outlook on life. Not that I didn't look straight into the deep dark recesses of a pit like the Rabbit Hole Alice fell into from *Alice in Wonderland*. At some seemingly hopeless moments, I wondered what this disease had brought into our lives and thought to myself, "What's the point of going on?" and "My life is over." Just in case you've ever thought that way, I encourage you to read the rest of my book, because even though friends and family express empathy for what you're going through, no one can fully understand unless if they've walked in your shoes.

You are not alone. There is hope for a future with happiness. You will survive this and be a better person because of it. Follow some of my tried-and-true strategies for survival and – even though you didn't sign up for this role in your life – you will be able to reflect on your journey and appreciate lessons-learned, knowing you gave a gift of yourself to your loved one, without losing yourself.

REFLECTION
YOUR TURN

Journaling is an important survival mechanism and I encourage you to try it for the first time if you've never tried it before. Feel free to write down your true, most meaningful feelings to get the most out of this strategy for survival.

1. *Remember the day your life changed forever when you realized that dementia in your family member wasn't going away. Write down as many details about this moment that you can. Where were you? What did you feel? What things did you feel you were losing? Were there any positive relationships or situations that were helpful to you?*

   _____

   _____

   _____

   _____

   _____

   _____

   _____

2. *Gratitude is integral in surviving any challenging situation. With gratitude, abundance will follow. Write down three things you are grateful for right now in your life and why:*

   _____

   _____

   _____

   _____

   _____

   _____

   _____

Chapter 2

Early Signs

Of course, each situation will vary, so I can only share what I went through from my viewpoint while I watched my husband fall deeper into the horrifying world of dementia. Like many other men in his early 60's, he was not a very technological person, and anything that had to do with technology he would avoid and not really do anything with. He was one of the old hanger-outs to have the old "flip phone" and never sent an email or text. Any efforts to teach him a new technology skill or any new skill were rejected. This was definitely one of the early signs.

My husband's problems were compounded because he was a heavy beer drinker (born and raised in Chicago) who turned to alcohol in times of loss. Loss in the form of death had been an unwanted constant in his life. His job opportunities in his late 50's became limited, and he was spending more and more time alone at home. I noticed he became much more regimented in certain things and he ate the same things every day for breakfast, lunch and dinner and you may notice that in your person as well. Every morning, he had his Raisin Bran Cereal and for lunch a salad and peanut butter and jelly sandwich and dinner varied because I made them. His doctor told me that he had to lose weight, so he did get more health conscious and began taking walks every day and did cut down on his beer drinking.

Other early signs included his loss of math computations. This was a man who could add up figures in his head without ever using a calculator. He did our taxes every year which included home expenses and a couple of small businesses. It was around this time that I knew he could never do our taxes again. So, I took that upon myself. First, I worked with my daughter-in-law and then I went to a tax company. As a caregiver, you will see that, little bit by little bit, anything that your loved one oversaw suddenly becomes your responsibility to take on. For example, he always did the grass cutting, which I must admit I pretty much took for granted, and I should have appreciated it more than I did because now it's costing me $100 a cut to get my lawn done! So, it was just like he didn't really know how to get the mower started and he didn't remember if he put oil in it. He never seemed to have the gas, so he just wasn't doing that, so that went by the way side. Also, I found myself bringing the large garbage cans and recyclables to the street all the time. That had always been his job – to put the garbage cans out by the curb on the correct pick up days. So, more and more, these jobs became my responsibility.

In his late 50's, he got a job driving for Connection Bus, which transported handicapped people. (Sadly, and ironically, we used this service to transport him in his wheelchair for home visits.) He had always been an excellent driver and he had a superb sense of direction. He had no problem at that time navigating where he was supposed to be going to. Some days he was up at 5 a.m. in the morning to be able to pick up his client and get him to his location without GPS by just using a map. However, when that business turned to using iPad technology where he'd have to check in and out and track his trips – that's when he put in his 2-week notice. I would ask, "How did it work out with the iPad?" and he'd say, "It just didn't work today," and he kept blaming it on the iPad. Finally, we both kind of knew that it was him having the problem, not the iPad.

I guess we kind of hid our heads in the sand around this time. We knew that something was going on, but our lives were still manageable, we were okay, and to think of the worst was more than we wanted to do. My career at that point was probably at its highest than it had ever been: I was publishing teen books and was recently named "Teacher of the Year" for Palm Beach County, so while my career had probably been at its highest point, everything with my career had to take the back burner. The whole focus of my energy was on my husband, helping him navigate what he was going to be experiencing.

My sister-in-law, who saw what her parents and his parents had to go through, (they both had dementia, the mother had Alzheimer's and the father had alcohol-related dementia) insisted I take him to a doctor for a full write-up of mental and memory testing and I remember that both my husband and I felt that she was intruding into our lives. We did succumb to her wishes, however, because experts suggest that early diagnosis is extremely important and recommend getting on a drug such as "Aricept," which he did. Perhaps it did help a little because Mike did have a few pretty good years. Plus, there's so many things that go along with this disease that require time and the cooperation of your loved one: getting your affairs in order, preferable by a lawyer who has the extra distinction of understanding elder affairs to create a living will, trusts, power of attorney forms, etc. So, at that point we did see a lawyer to create our Monroe Family Trust, Power of Attorney forms, Medical Power of Attorney forms, Living Will, etc.

I'll never forget our first initial screenings. We went to St. Mary's Hospital for a screening for dementia where they did separate testing/consultations for Mike and other family members. I attended with my two grown daughters, and we let loose and cried a little bit talking about some of the things we noticed going on. Then, we went to a neurologist, who specialized in dementia, where my husband did the famous "Draw a clock at 10 minutes after 4 o clock," and "How many 4-legged animals can you name in one minute?" He failed both tests miserably.

During these sessions with Mike's neurologist, his explanations and answers to the doctor's questions weren't very thorough. This first doctor diagnosed him as having Alzheimer's. He was starting to have tremors at that time; it wasn't until we went to see a second neurologist that he was diagnosed with "Lewy Body Dementia," [**Lewy body dementia** (LBD) is a disease associated with abnormal deposits of a protein called alpha-synuclein in the brain. These deposits, called **Lewy bodies**, affect chemicals in the brain whose changes, in turn, can lead to problems with thinking, movement, behavior, and mood.]

Because of the tremors, Lewy Body Dementia is significantly different from Alzheimer's. (Imagine they are brothers in the same family of dementia.) Remember, any diagnosis of the type of dementia can only be 100 % accurate after death via a brain autopsy. Many patients have a condition called "Mixed dementia." [Note: We recently received the autopsy results from the Mount Sinai Brain Bank, and it stated, "The main pathological findings on Mr. Michael Monroe were those of: Diffuse Lewy Body Disease and Alzheimer's Disease. Both Lewy Body and Alzheimer pathology were widespread in the brain and most likely were together responsible for the initial and later symptoms and the progression of the disease." Amid great feelings of sadness while reading this report, our family still appreciated a definitive diagnosis of his disease.]

I remember the second neurologist had a weird way of speaking to me in front of my husband. For example, he held up a highlighter and said to me, "What color is this highlighter?" I answered, "It's yellow," and he said, "No, it's pink." And I said, "Well, I know you're trying to make some point and he said, "From now on, whatever he says is his reality. The only thing you say is, 'Yes, dear.'" And he said that will save you a lot of aggravation because there's no reason for you to try to correct him. Because that is his perception and it is true for him. That is something that has always stuck with me. I've never been much of a "Yes, dear," type of person, but I could see the point of not arguing with someone over something like that. That doctor also told me a weird story: "Poor Mrs. White. Her husband has Alzheimer's and will live with his disease for a long, long time. Then, there's Mrs. Green, whose husband has Lewy Body Disease. Her husband will live for 5 to 7 years with his disease." I never forgot that story. Ironically, it came through. Mike passed about six years after his first signs of his disease at 68.

Mike was a very easy-going person and took charge of most of his own care in the beginning. However, there was a subtle shifting with me having to oversee him making up his medicines; he couldn't be trusted with that. At this point, he was still staying at home when I went to work, and I would put signs on the door that said, "Mike, stay home. Do not go anywhere." We had a couple of weird instances where it seemed that he had been hallucinating because when we got home, he once charged at my daughter with a golf club in his hand, saying, "They're coming at us. They're coming at us." Mike was a veteran; he had been in the Army in the '70's during Vietnam, but he didn't go to Vietnam; he went to Germany. So, we thought he could be bringing up past memories from his Army days. They say the older memories are more firmly rooted in the brain, so it made sense. He also would look out the kitchen window to the home next to us and say, "That's where I was stationed when I was in the service." And it was of course our neighbor's house. These were all the beginning signs.

Still, when we went to bed at night, he seemed okay, he'd sleep okay. He'd wake up in the morning, no problem. At this point he was still showering for himself, shaving every day, dressing, and eating on his own.

I was trying to finish up my school year without having to make any big decisions, and then it came to my last day at school, when I was in line to check out with my principal (All teachers have a check-out list that you have to complete before you can leave for the summer) and one of his best friends got a phone call from him (he was still able to use the phone at that time) and he called me, and said that Mike sounds like he is very lost and upset and he said he took a walk and he doesn't know where your house is. So, I had to leave school immediately and by the time I got back to the house, he was just walking back into our yard. He always liked to carry a cooler or bag with stuff in it, so he had a bag filled with all sorts of stuff – pictures, underwear, gadgets; the bag was filled to the brim with all these items. He was sweating, and I brought him into the house, calmed him down, gave him a glass of water, and that's when I realized he couldn't be left alone any more. And that's when I made the decision for him to go to an adult day care center while I was at work. So, I was off for that summer and I was able to make those decisions before I needed to return to work the following school year. It was also the summer that I planned our last big vacation together: a trip to Hawaii, which was quite difficult, but as I look back at my decision, I'm happy that we shared this once-in-a-lifetime experience together. The photos of us on the Hawaiian beaches still warm my heart.

REFLECTION
YOUR TURN

1. *Write down the early signs of dementia that you are either seeing now in your loved one, or you remember happening in the past. These early signs were the turning point that might have spurred you to action to get help or a diagnosis for your loved one:*

    _____

    _____

    _____

    _____

    _____

    _____

    _____

2. *How did you feel about these early signs? Did you feel a shift where you had to make decisions for another adult, having new responsibilities for another human being?*

    _____

    _____

    _____

    _____

    _____

    _____

    _____

Chapter 3

Can't Leave Him Alone

*T*his is probably one of the biggest turning points in a caregiver's life. It usually involves trying to find some type of care that either comes into the home, staying home with your loved one, or bringing them to an adult day care. In my case, I had a retirement program for about three more years in my position as a high school English teacher that I needed to complete for my financial security and so it necessitated that I continue to work. Plus, I know for me, I would not be able to be a 7-days-a-week, 24-hours-a-day caregiver. I applaud those who are caregivers in that capacity and anyone who is in a caregiving role deserves the most props ever. However, for me, I needed to find a place that I could afford that he could go to. So, since my husband was a veteran, I did reach out to my VA social worker and the only place that was approved for the Veteran Association paying for his care of three times a week was the Alzheimer's Community Care Center at a local church.

My first impression of going there was shocking: I imagined seeing where my husband might end up in a year because you see so many people in wheelchairs and so many people barely able to function and communicate. All the workers that I have encountered in these roles are angels on Earth because it is not an easy job; it's so exhausting. Although I didn't see a very high level of one-on-one personalized enrichment programs, they did try to provide as entertaining of an environment that you can have for a large group of people in that situation.

One other facility that I really liked that had more speakers coming in, more crafts and different things like that, was not approved by the Veteran's Association even though the facility was far superior. If you know anything about the Veteran's Association, it's a slow process. The manager of that facility had been going through the process for VA approval for many months, but still was not approved.

So, Mike started going to the Alzheimer's Association Community Care Center, a place where he attended for two full years with much success. They outfitted him with an electronic monitoring device that could locate him if he wandered off. I also learned about a wonderful service in my community for the handicapped – Connection Bus Service, and I enrolled him in that program, so I wouldn't have to drive him to and from the facility and still try to work at my teaching job. This service was, ironically, the same company that my husband used to work for. So, for $7 a day, I could get them to pick up my husband from my home and take him to the place. He looked forward to the rides and I think it was a blessing that he had worked for them before because he thought he was going "to work."

Of course, with any service like Adult Day Care, you are going to have to do a ton of paperwork: forms to fill out, prescriptions in original bottles with the original prescriptions from doctors, so they could administer any medications he would normally be taking during the day. As for the bus service, I had to get a code for him and reserve his pick-up times on a weekly basis until they would let me have an ongoing "standing order" schedule. You had to be ready and flexible because the bus could be up to one half hour before or after your selected time.

They try to keep Adult Day Cares as clean as possible, but when you walk into those places, there is a certain odor, that, unfortunately, is pretty much unavoidable. In this case, it wasn't the smell of urine, it was the smell of strong Lysol; since it was in a church recreational area, the church people probably used a strong cleaning agent to clean it every day. So, it has a distinctive smell; when you bring your loved one home, his clothes, hair and skin have that distinctive smell. It's something you just have to get used to and make him take a shower right away and wash his clothes every day.

I was lucky with my husband; he liked going there and he liked driving on the bus, because he was familiar with it. I think he liked the social interaction after being home alone so long. In fact, he was quite popular with some of the lady guests there because he was tall and he always wore a ball cap and the ladies would walk around with him and hold his hand. The caregivers said that he reminded them of their husbands. The caregivers would say, "He's quite popular because he's a nice guy, very friendly and the ladies relate to his ball cap because their husbands also wore them."

I had a couple of incidents where he was low on blood pressure and they had to rush him to the emergency room, but then he was fine. We also had a few occasions where he was getting on the aggressive side where he refused to do the table activities and once wiped a puzzle completely off the table in an angry gesture. Another time, they wanted him to color and he didn't want to color, so he would knock the crayons and coloring book off the table, which is totally unlike his normal personality. But that is what you can expect with this disease — that this aggressiveness will come out. You can only imagine what's going on in their minds. This is the very cruelest of diseases.

So, we did that for about two years, and grew accustomed to the wonderful caregivers. Unfortunately, in that line of work, the pay isn't that good and there was quite a bit of turnover. Just when you'd get used to one nursing assistant and you would bond with that worker and talk to her about your loved one, she would be gone and you'd have to start all over with another. They provided the free locator bracelet, and he, like the other ones in the facility, would try to escape when someone would get picked up. They used a loud buzzer system when the outer door opened and closed with a code. So, if someone tried to leave with you, it was up to the hard-working attendant to say, "No, no, sit down. It's not your turn yet to leave."

They tried their best to make a family-like experience for the caregivers: we had a Thanksgiving Dinner that my daughters and I were able to attend, as well as a "Caregivers are Superheroes" event, which was really special. They had a wonderful first-class annual Caregivers' banquet, where they asked me to be the Caregiver speaker, which I was very honored to do, to pay tribute to the workers and other caregivers who work so hard every day, working with these people in this horrible situation. In my talk, I stressed how this disease is not just the person's disease, but also the caregiver's disease and the whole family's disease. I talked about how this disease can take one of you or both of you, so you must guard your heart, your soul, your spirit, so you're not an unlikely victim to this disease, which is not his fault, which is not your fault. It is a cruel, heartless disease.

I tried to make the best of these two years. Mike was still ambulatory and enjoyed going to a restaurant and even having one beer. (That was all he was allowed by his doctor.) I would sometimes cancel his bus trip home and pick him up and then take us to a local restaurant or to a movie to treat ourselves. For a few brief moments, we could make time stand still, we could still be Mike and Mary.

That spring and summer of 2017 was the first time I tried the idea of "respite," whereby the caregiver gets the chance to get an uninterrupted time away for the purposes of vacation, or in my case, a free teacher seminar in Pennsylvania with the Medal of Honor Foundation. They have many different caregiver options for "respite," whereby you can leave your loved one in a facility for a week or two to get a break, and the VA or Medicaid would pay for it. The only problem with these respite opportunities is that you won't know literally until 24 hours before you need to leave if there will be a bed available! So, it makes it very, very difficult to even try to use these resources unless if your plans are extremely flexible. I did use it the one time at a local nursing facility with a very high rating. The dementia patients, however, were on the upstairs floor, separated from all of the exciting activities happening downstairs. Nevertheless, I did all of the necessary paperwork and thought I'd give it a try. I wasn't going out of town; I was staying in town and needed to get some things done. I brought my husband in walking and somewhat coherent and three days later when I picked him up, he was all curled up in a wheelchair and all hunched over on one side and I said, "What did you do in three days to my husband?" and "Can I see a record of what medications he was on?" and they pretty much told me very little and made it very difficult for me to find out any information. I took him home, barely getting him in and out of the car, and then I put him in the shower and his body was curled over in a 90-degree angle. I laid him out on the bed and got a mound of lotion and basically ironed him out to try to get him straight again. It took him about two days to be able to stand up straight in the shower again. So, that was not a good experience. So, I looked for other options for respite for the Medal of Honor teacher educational trip. I finally chose the option of a live-in aide who stayed in my home round-the-clock while I was on this trip. This turned out to be a much better option for me. To use this option, you must be able to: 1. Put all of your valuables and papers in a safe locked place. Earlier in the year, I had purchased a large safe from Costco and had it mounted to the floor of my garage. 2. Feel comfortable with someone living in your home, sleeping in one of your home's beds, and being 100% responsible for your loved one. To work up to this option, for several weeks prior, as I stated before, I had taken advantage of the VA's program, whereby they provide a home health aide to come into your home, shower, shave, dress and feed your loved one – up to 10 times a week. (If you do not have VA care, this care is about $25 an hour, depending on where you live.) At first, I thought I didn't need the help, it's not necessary, but then I thought, "What the heck. Let me try it." It wasn't too awfully bad in the beginning. Unfortunately, you never got the same person. If you were lucky, you'd get the same person for several weeks. So, the person would get him showered, dressed, put on his deodorant, supervise his breakfast, so that was very helpful, so I could get myself ready for my job as a teacher, overseeing a hundred high school teenagers a day, teaching reading, writing and grammar! It took some of the pressure off of me because I'd always have to get him ready first, then get me ready, and then make sure the bus picked him up in time for me to get to my job!

Things changed when I had to resume my school year beginning in the Fall, 2017. I had new courses to teach and it necessitated that I had to be at work every other day at 7:30 a.m. This caused problems because we had been accustomed to having help in the mornings for Mike to get ready.

The VA was providing up to one hour every morning for a home health aide to come to our house and help Mike shower, shave, get dressed, etc.

We had two wonderful, wonderful caregivers who walked into our lives at that time that I will never forget. The one lady, originally from Jamaica, a spirited woman, immediately took charge of the situation and showed an incredible respect to my husband. Since she knew he was in the Army, she'd address him like this: "Soldier, soldier, it's time to get up, soldier. The troops are waiting. You must report to duty." And one day he was a sergeant and one day he was a captain. And I said to her, "Pretty soon, he's going to be President of the United States. He gets a different promotion every week." He responded so well to her. If he was sluggish and didn't want to get up, she'd said, "Captain, the troops are waiting for your commands. It's important for you to get up." His body was getting stiff from the Lewy Body Dementia, but she was great — she took the time to put body lotion all over his arms and legs, so his skin was in very good condition. We made him a big breakfast every day and most days he left for the adult day care in a very good spirit on the bus. The hardest thing was losing her without too much of an explanation; apparently, someone else she worked for needed her 24-7. One day, she simply did not show up. We felt such a loss. So then, it was one new girl after another new girl after another new girl until it seemed that it would be easier for me to just get him ready myself. The problem was that most of these aides had full time jobs elsewhere and the agencies didn't pay them well enough to come and do a 1-hour job from 6:30 to 7:30, since I needed to leave early for my job at the high school. Plus, many of these hard-working individuals were trying to become RN's, so they were going to school at night. The agencies would only pay them for the one-hour of care, about $12, with no additional money for travel and the one aide shared with me that her agency dropped all pay $6 an hour when new ownership came in. They had been making $18 an hour, and the new owners moved them down, all to $12 an hour. I could totally empathize — who would wake up super early, get dressed, get their own families and children ready for school and work, leave their own home to care for a handicapped man and then on top of it get paid $12 an hour and use their own gas?

I kept in touch for some time with another very good caregiver who came to the house who was getting her nursing degree. Many people do not trust caregivers to come into their home; they fear they will steal jewelry or money from them. I can just say, from my own experience, since all of my aides were from an approved agency, which was licensed and insured, that I was never aware of any of these situations in my home. Prior to this time, as I stated before, I invested in a very large "gun" safe (even though it wasn't for guns) with a digital code and twist lock on it. I had a handyman bolt it into the floor of my garage and I ordered online a cover for it, which gives it the appearance of a wood cabinet. Into this safe, I put any valuables, papers with social security numbers on them, jewelry, coins, etc. As I stated before, these women are just trying to earn a living and they would lose their jobs if they stole from their clients. It was not a problem for me.

We continued with this home care in the mornings for several weeks, often having a new girl every other day, until I had to make that all-important decision to place my husband in an assisted living or nursing home facility. I could not have him continue going to the Adult Day Care anymore and continue at my job. The morning routine confusion and chaos was taking a toll on all of us. I considered quitting my job or even taking a medical leave to stay at home with him, but common sense ruled against this option. The financial loss for me to stay home with him was too great, plus I knew mentally I wouldn't be a "perfect" caregiver to stay at home with him. (Note: I remember someone told me to never strive to be an A caregiver. You'll drive yourself crazy. Just aim to be a C caregiver or even a C minus. You will be a little kinder to yourself that way.)

It finally got to the point that we had a horrible hurricane here in Florida, Hurricane Irma, that made landfall September 10, and we were without electricity for 8 days and the Day Care facility was closed as well. It's hard to explain to a person with dementia why he can't watch TV, why it's so hot, why it's dark at night. He was getting a little aggressive, not sleeping as well at night, and getting up during the night and urinating in corners of the room and making it very difficult to handle him at home. So, a family decision was made to put him into either an assisted living facility or a nursing home for dementia patients. This process had been going on and off for the last six months, and every time I found a pretty decent facility, there was either no bed available, or you were told you had to wait for someone to die. And the person who had to die had to be the same sex as your loved one! We went around and around until I was dizzy from the whole thing.

I had been doing research about nursing home and assisted living facilities for the past several months, visiting places to see if I could find one that I could afford. The admissions woman at one facility, which had a very high ranking, told me it's not best to bring him here until he's not sure who's sitting across from him at the dinner table. I really didn't like her attitude either; she acted like her facility was a business, and it was the first time I heard the saying, "Head to bed." She would lose money any day of the week she didn't have a paying "head to bed." At that time, I gave her a $549 check as a deposit and made plans for my husband to move there. During our conversations, I told her that my husband did occasionally have the habit of getting up in the middle of the night and peeing in a corner of the room; she told me that he'd have to room with another "pee-er" and she'd have to order a straight-jacket type of garment for him to wear at night, whereby he couldn't undress himself to pee during the night! Plus, I'd have to pay for it out-of-pocket! She actually showed me the room to see if I was bothered by any scent of urine, so when we went to that room, she sniffed around and said to me, "See, it's not too bad. Not too bad at all. This should work for you. Don't you agree?" At that point, I went back to her office, grabbed up my deposit check, and ran out of the building!

But during the week right before Hurricane Irma, I went to Florida's state VA nursing home in Broward County where they said they would take his social security money and his VA money and after I painstakingly filled out a packet of 36 pages, she told me that I would have to apply for Medicaid and I explained to her that I already had Medicaid for him and we just needed to switch from community care to nursing home care, and I even put my representative, whom I had a very nice relationship with, on the phone with her who told her that I already qualified and it would just be switched over. The VA representative told me that his application of 36 pages could move no further until I applied, so the next day during my break at work, I went online and quickly applied for nursing home Medicaid and made a mistake on my application which cost me three months of uncertainty and confusion because on the "online" version, there was no place to say that he had a "Medicaid trust account," which we had set up, so he was denied. So, a lot of the red tape at these nursing homes can cause you big problems if not done correctly. I did not go to an elder law attorney to help me with these applications, which can cost you up to $7,000. I did my paperwork myself with the help of a caring woman at my local Aging Council, who was terrific. She guided me through my Medicaid application, but again, it was not an easy process. There was even a particular problem with that VA hospital where they made a home visit and the male social worker ripped up a necessary form that came from my local VA hospital social worker. He said that my husband had to be evaluated for a mental disorder or anxiety since he had a prescription for Alprazolam (commonly known as Zanex) for his tremors, and he wrote up a new form and the whole thing struck me as a little fishy; well it turned out that form was thrown out upon review, and this further delayed his acceptance in the VA nursing facility. Nothing had been processed yet for my husband at the VA hospital, so he could not be admitted.

I was at my wit's end when I threw myself out to God and the Universe, pleading for help, and miraculously I came upon an ad for a Finnish Rest Home Nursing facility right near my local Costco! I made a phone call and this caring loving woman came on the phone and said, "Yes, we have an opening for your husband. It will be in a day or two when the air conditioning comes on" (since they had lost their electricity in the Hurricane too). And it was like the heavens opened up, because I was at my last straw – the nine days of no electricity, trying to navigate him at night with just flashlights and lanterns, and I finally had a place to bring my husband to, which brought us to a whole new realm in our journey, caring for my husband outside the home in a nursing facility.

Unfortunately, this stay was only for about four weeks, because my husband had two aggressive incidents: he grabbed the sides of a wheelchair with the patient inside of it and stormed very fast at the doors in an "escape" move. After a second incident of him actually hitting one of the male attendants, he was kicked out! I was devastated. It was Oct. 11, 2017 and it was his 68th birthday. The caring woman at the Finnish Home said that she was recommending a special Assisted Living Facility specifically designed for Dementia patients. The owner of this facility met with me and I signed the paperwork for his transfer sight unseen. I had to trust these two individuals because I was literally at the end of my rope. I made the decision to put him in the least expensive of the rooming options, with 3 other roommates. It was still going to be $3,300 monthly, but with expected aid, should cost me about $1,950 a month. That day, his birthday, my daughters and I packed him up from the one facility and brought him to the other one, where he lived until his death on July 22, 2018. Through the grace of God, that place had been wonderful to him and is filled with loving caregivers who truly care for their patients. He went through Hospice there for several months, as his disease had progressed to the point that he was in a wheelchair, unable to no longer walk or really communicate in a meaningful way. The facility allowed us to bring him home most Sundays to be with his family. It was all part of our "new normal," a normal no one in their right mind would ever sign up for or wish on their worst enemy.

REFLECTION
YOUR TURN

There will probably come a time (or has already come) that you will need additional help for your loved one, where they can't be left alone. Prior planning prevents poor performance. Here's a checklist for you to consider:

- *Have you visited day care facilities in your area? Have you looked for community resources to help with the costs?*
- *Have you applied for Medicaid or VA benefits? You can seek a lawyer who specializes in elder affairs for assistance. It will be worth your time and money. There are also free services available. Seek out your local aging council.*
- *Have you visited assisted living facilities and nursing homes? Many will require that you leave information for a "waiting list." In your journal, consider the following: When did you realize that you needed outside help? This required a shift in your mental outlook on the situation. How were you feeling about this change in your journey with your loved one suffering with dementia? Please be honest with yourself.*

_____

_____

_____

_____

Chapter 4

Family Feuds

$\mathscr{C}$hildhood insecurities and rivalries that had long been put to rest can come back in full force and raise their ugly heads when a group of siblings have to come together to determine the upcoming care of a family member, dad, or mom, in the face of impending dementia. Often it is the females in the family who bear the majority of work when it comes to caregiving for a parent. This puts an unfair burden on women who probably are largely involved with the many tasks of family, career, and middle-aged health issues.

The situation can become more complicated when family properties, the family home or inheritances that will be divided up between siblings have consequences regarding the care of the family member. For example, one person told me that her father had worked hard his whole life to provide an inheritance of $250,000 for herself and her two sisters. When her father got Alzheimer's and started to become too much work for her mother (who was used to the finer things in life), her mother immediately put her husband in a nursing home for the duration of his illness, which was seven years. The cost of his care, (which can be up to $7,000 a month) dwindled away a lot of the savings. In addition, since this person lived in another state, she was unable to watch too closely as her older sister moved into the family home with her three children and lived rent-free for many years. Lavish trips were enjoyed by the mother and this daughter and were paid for by the mother's savings. The older sister had also changed the title on the family home to include her own name with right of survivorship upon the death of either. After the father died, very little savings were left, and then when the mother died, her sister got the home. After procuring a lawyer, she ended up with a very small amount of money and a divided family for the rest of her life. She and her sister never spoke again.

It is best to see a lawyer who specializes in elder affairs, who can advise you and your family on the best way to protect assets and property. The investment will pay for itself a hundred times over! Our family home was put in a trust with all three of my children as co-executors. As my husband lost his decision-making abilities, it was necessary to remove him as a trustee of the estate. Even though we did this, I was told that because of Florida law, if I had passed before my husband, he still would have had the home go entirely to him instead of my children, who would then monitor it for him. I didn't feel comfortable with it set up like this, but I was told that was Florida law! The law and estates are quite complicated. Please seek out advice, so you will not be a victim of a situation of another case such as this: a father could no longer live in a manufactured home in a small town in Florida near his son, who was his primary caregiver. A daughter brought him into her home and retired to take care of him for over a year. She had assumed that the brother had taken care of all of the legal paperwork and will for her dad, and only became aware that no legal paperwork for her father had been done until he needed intensive care for a condition brought on as a consequence of his Alzheimer's. It became a logistic nightmare to get the proper paperwork in order before his death, and it left behind a scarred and fragmented family.

Please do not assume that paperwork has been done. Ask to see it if someone else in the family is in charge. In this case, a parent never sent back the paperwork to the lawyer with unsettling effects: a woman cared for a father-in-law for many, many years throughout his dementia. Right before he was able to make any of his own decisions, she found that he had never signed any of the paperwork that his lawyer had sent to him (and oddly the lawyer had never followed up on it either.) Consequently, she helped him finalize the paperwork and took it upon herself to cut out one of the siblings from the inheritance who had not been around to help with the father's care! The disinherited son and her husband are estranged to this day.

Families that were once strong can break under the pressure of handling a parent's affairs. For instance, there was the case of a very close family of three siblings: a son and two daughters. The mother had put her youngest daughter as her power of attorney. When the mother had to be put in a nursing home and the youngest daughter could no longer take care of paying the taxes, insurance and care for the family home, she sold it at a fraction of what it was worth to one of her male friends. When her brother offered to buy the home for the same price she was selling it to her male friend, he tried to talk and convince his mother to let him buy the family home, but she had been convinced that he was not to be trusted (not true) and the house went for a 50% sale price to the sister's friend. That money was quickly gobbled up by the nursing home and the once close family was left fragmented to this day. (The "friend" who purchased the home "flipped it" and made himself a handsome profit!)

You will find that some family members are very comfortable visiting their loved ones once they are put in a facility, and others are reluctant to the point that visiting the loved one in a nursing home or assisted living facility gives them such anxiety and pain that they avoid it altogether. This is compounded by the fact that Alzheimer's can have a genetic risk for the children of the afflicted, so when a son or daughter refuses to visit dad or mom in the facility, they are trying to avoid seeing into their possible future. This can cause resentment for the family members who visit regularly despite having their own jobs and family responsibilities.

I'm sure you have heard about these stories over and over again. Here are some tips so your family doesn't become victim to these inevitable decisions that have a huge impact on finances and relationships:

1. Early on, get proper legal advice and paperwork drafted by a lawyer who specializes in estate and elder affairs. The cost of this work will pay for itself tenfold in later years. In my case, we drafted a "Monroe Family Trust," whereby all three of my grown children would be co-executors of our estate upon our passing.

2. Try to be as transparent as possible with all family members involved through emails, texts and other forms of communication. Problems can arise when family members believe a "conspiracy" is occurring and leaving them out.

3. Discuss and brainstorm major decisions before jumping to action. Other family members may offer you a valuable piece of information that you were not aware of. Try to put your "ego" aside and the urge to be "right" or mom and dad's "favorite" to respectively consider all points of view. Try to adapt a "We're all in this together," attitude.

4. If possible, find out the passing wishes of the loved one before they are unable to make these decisions. Do they want a funeral? A celebration of life? Do they want to be buried or cremated? Do they want to donate their body or brain tissue to science? Try to handle as many of these items before the inevitable to save yourself stress and money. How many people have unwittingly bought the most expensive (and most unnecessary) casket during a time of deep emotion that left them in debt for years? In my case with my husband, I learned about Florida's "Brain Bank," at a Caregiver's Seminar, whereby my husband's brain tissue will be used to further research to find a cure for dementia. Although I wrestled with this idea for many months, after talking to the person in charge of the program, I got my husband accepted into it. One benefit is that my children will be provided with a free autopsy report, specifically labeling the types of dementia he had, thus allowing them knowledge about any potential genetic risks to them or their children.

5. Consider the purchase of a $5,000 or $10,000 Life Insurance Policy to cover burial expenses. There are several available without any medical questions. If the loved one dies before a certain number of years, you can get back the money that was put into it. I had

this for my husband, and it did pay the monies I paid in since it didn't reach the length of term required.

6. Come together as much as possible as a team with the same purpose in mind: to provide the best, most compassionate care within financial means for your loved one. Be lavish with praise to the other family members, short with criticism, and pat yourself on the back often too. This journey is not one that any of us signed up for and it can tax you to your last breath but stay steadfast and finish through to the end with dignity and respect. You and your family can survive this. After all, that is what your loved one would want.

REFLECTION
YOUR TURN

Write down some of the ways your family worked as a team in this journey down the Dementia pit. Then, write down some incidents where you or a family member felt hurt or disrespected during decisions that had to be made.

_____

_____

_____

_____

Is there anything you can do now to build a bridge to solve a family problem that has occurred during the care of your loved one? If so, write it down here, and then do it!

_____

_____

_____

_____

Chapter 5

Organization is Key

$\mathscr{A}$re you an organized person? If you are, then this next part of your life's journey as a caregiver will just come naturally to you. If you aren't, then this may be a good time to put some tried-and-true practices into place to make your life easier.

For me, I was what I'd like to call a "pile" organizer. Instead of neat files in a file cabinet (even though I had one of those), I found that I had "piles" of information related to caregiving. One pile might be on his medical plan, one pile might be all the utility bills I needed to submit to qualify for aid, one pile might be brochures on different nursing homes and assisted living facilities and one pile might be caregiver groups and services! Sometimes I put the "piles" into light bags: the Publix grocery bag had all of the nursing homes, the slim backpack had all of the bills, etc. This was found to be **NOT**, I repeat **NOT**, the most efficient or organized method because somehow those bags always got mis-located: I'd take one to the VA hospital and forget it in the car, etc.

Here's some tips and advice I'd like to share about getting organized when you're a caregiver. Some may be basic, some may give you an "Ah ha" moment, and some may just get you motivated.

1. De-clutter your home. Prior to my husband's diagnosis, I was a weekly participant in going to "garage sales." Consequently, I had way too many knick-knacks, multiple kitchen serving dishes, gadgets, etc. Try to streamline your living space as much as possible to make it functional. The dementia patient when living at home needs a routine to provide a sense of security. Safety for your loved one should be a top priority. Get rid of all throw rugs that are slip and fall hazards. If you have a swimming pool, get a baby guard fence. We have a swimming pool, and I did purchase and put up a baby fence that offers security through locked gates, and this came in handy to protect Mike as well. Around the middle stages of Mike's dementia, we invested in an electric gate around the front of our property. It was well worth the money! Not only does it come in handy for keeping the grandchildren safe when playing in the yard, it offered me a sense of security that Mike couldn't wander off because he couldn't master the clickers to open the gates. Also, when driving back to our home after an avalanche of doctor and specialist appointments, it was so nice to not have to get out of the car to open the manual gate we used to have – especially in one of Florida's famous rain downfalls.

    Organize your closets and drawers and simplify clothes. There will be clothes that your loved one will no longer wear because of complicated buttons, long sleeves that are difficult to put on, pants and jeans that are too big because of weight loss. Bag them up and donate immediately to a worthy cause. Do the same with your own clothes. Organize your drawers so you can find your underwear, workout clothes, career clothes, and comfy pajamas easily so you don't get frustrated, trying to work through piles of disorganized clothes.

    Do laundry almost daily, or whenever it fits in your schedule.

The clothes from an Adult Day Care will have an odor to them. Use your usual laundry detergent or add vinegar to your wash to freshen any smell of urine.

Once my husband became incontinent, I was doing a load of laundry almost every morning. Although he was wearing Depends at night, for some reason, he had so much urine by morning, it leaked onto the sheets, bed pad and other linens – even though I protected the mattress with a (supposedly) waterproof mattress pad, followed by a large industrial strength black garbage bag, and multiple disposable pads (and I tried one sturdy washable one as well.) The problem is you can't explain to a person with dementia that he needs to sleep on the disposable pads! On many mornings, the pads were all wadded up and wet in the bed, with urine soaking through everything. Of course, that would necessitate me stripping the bed and throwing a load in the washer before I went to work! I finally researched on YouTube the best way to get the urine smell out of linens: plain vinegar. Once the water fills in your washing machine, you add a cup of vinegar to your regular laundry detergent before putting in the sheets, mattress pad, etc. That was the only way that the clothes didn't smell like urine, even after they were washed with detergent.

2. Organize toiletries and grooming items in your bathroom. You need to make your bathroom an efficiency workroom. My husband was able to shave for quite a while, brush his teeth and shower on his own. But, as the disease progressed, I had to learn how to shave a man's beard and mustache area, apply his deodorant, comb his hair, brush his teeth, floss his teeth, etc. Having a plentiful supply of grooming items handy made this unwanted task a bit easier. Once incontinence became an issue, I needed to make sure that I always had gloves handy for body contact, plenty of disposable wipes or heavier wipes that would have to be wadded up and discarded. Your large white kitchen bags become indispensable, and an investment in bathroom and bedroom garbage cans with the automatic sealable lids are a very welcome addition to your routine. (Baby diaper pails may work well too.) Take the trash out often to keep your sleeping area as pleasant as possible. And don't

forget the Febreze or the toilet product that goes into the bowl before toileting. Before I could teach my husband to sit to urinate (not an easy task for a man who has stood to urinate for over 50 years) I needed to keep on hand a roll of antiseptic cleaning cloths to wipe down the toilet seat, and around the toilet because he often sprayed urine all over the seat because he either forgot to lift it or the tremors from his disease would shake his penis when he was urinating! Not fun!

3.   Organize paperwork. One very unwelcome part of being a caregiver is the mountains and mountains of paperwork that you will oversee. The first big category is legal paperwork, your Power of Attorney forms that cover finances, Medical Advance Health Care Directive (Durable Power of Attorney for Healthcare) forms (these forms are often used to decide on feeding tubes, ventilators, and other treatments at the end of life, including the DNR form — Do Not Resuscitate), Living Will, and Trust Originals. The earlier you get these forms completed the better, because the forms must be completed while your loved one is competent to know what he or she is signing, ie: without dementia. Also, check to see if your name is on all of your utility bills. I still have bills in my husband's name and need to change them now, which is quite a hassle!

Every time you enroll your loved one in a special medical program, see a new doctor or specialist, enroll in Adult Day Care or a Live-in facility, you will receive a mountain of paperwork, including brochures, copies of forms you signed, etc. Here's some tips for handling this: process the materials the same day you receive them. I invested in a large box of manila folders with clasps. They are big enough to hold all of the papers, brochures, etc. I clearly label with marker across the top in the same spot the contents of the envelope and the date I received them and store in a hanging file rolling cart I found at a garage sale. The point is to find a system that works for you. Maybe you would work best with colorful file folders and a filing cabinet with a lock on it. (Remember, a lot of these forms contain personal information about your loved one like their social security number, etc., so if you will have "strangers" in your home, you don't want to leave personal paperwork around to be easily assessible.) The most important points are to process the paperwork promptly upon receipt and to keep them in categories. It will all begin to blur together if you don't.

4.   Contacts and appointments. Invest in whatever tools you desire to make this unpleasant task easier for yourself. I always keep a wall calendar with appointments in my kitchen, with a back up day planner and appointments posted in my calendar on my I-Phone. I also immediately take a photo of important contact information and also enter it into my phone contacts on my IPhone, along with address information, and even directions if it's an odd place to find. I use the map app as well, but also get verbal directions to the offices because they are often on a certain floor, around a corner of a business address, etc. This punctual noting of appointments and contacts far outweighs scribbled notes on receipts or scraps of paper. Although I took down much information in that manner (scribbling info on scraps of paper in my purse) I try to quickly transfer my hieroglyphics into language I can read and access later! I kept a #10 envelope in my car filled with pertinent information on Mike, including his medications, copy of my power of attorney form, DNR, etc. in case of emergencies.

     I also found a large 4-inch notebook in my classroom that I brought home and placed a copy of all pertinent information on Mike in it. I hole-punched papers and placed in the 3-ring binder. If for some reason I was out of town or his paperwork had to be accessed quickly, it was all located in that one central place. I kept it in an obvious place where my family members all knew of its location.

5.   Medications. This is one of the most demanding tasks to keep on top of. As the caregiver, you need to keep a copy of the original prescription from the doctor as it may be necessary for Day Cares, respite, etc. Then, you need to come up with a system of renewing prescriptions that works for you. I had to order my husband's meds from the VA, which had a very specific method of ordering that you needed to follow. I also had other medications from other

doctors that I received from my local Walgreens on auto-renewal. Invest in a quality 7-day pill dispenser; they come in various types. Choose the one that suits you. Some are large with spots for pills that must be given at different times. I chose to have two of the simple 7-day containers: one for morning and one for night. I kept separate bottles for any other mid-day pills he needed to take. It worked for me. Find the system that works for you. Whatever you choose, it's best to fill the containers weekly on a day that is convenient for you. Be "mindful" when you do this task, so you don't accidentally make a mistake. It is quite easy to do when you have several things on your mind. I was rather annoyed with some of the prescriptions that he received from the VA that had to be cut in half for his dosage. I invested in a combination pill cutter and pill smasher device from Walgreens, so I had to cut those pills before I put them in his 7-day organizer, and eventually, I had to smash up all of his medications and mix with apple sauce or chocolate pudding because he was having problems swallowing his pills. Make sure you keep all medications out of the reach and eyesight of your loved one, just like you would for a child. When you're not looking, they could try to mimic you and take the whole bottle. Also, keep all medications away from visiting grandchildren, who have been known to be curious about pills, thinking they are candy.

To sum up, proper organization is key to your survival as a caregiver for your loved one with dementia. If you are not a "tidy" or organized person (many creative people aren't) give yourself permission to hire a professional. These services can be found through the internet and they promise to help you streamline your home, possessions, and paperwork. Other housecleaning services might give you the weekly deep cleaning break you need and deserve. These services could prove to be a well worth investment with multiple benefits for your peace of mind. Whether you do it yourself, or get professional help, pledge now to put your affairs in order. It is the best gift you can give to yourself and your loved one with dementia.

REFLECTION
YOUR TURN

1. *Look around your home and take note of any areas of uncleanliness or disorganization. Write them down here:*

_____

_____

_____

_____

_____

_____

_____

2. *What specific steps will you take to fix these areas of concern and discomfort? When will you do them? Imagine the effect of putting these steps in motion immediately and then do it! Write it down here:*

_____

_____

_____

_____

_____

_____

_____

Chapter 6

Attitude is Everything

A spiritual friend offered this advice, "Praise through the storm." Now, more than ever before, you must guard your mind from wallowing in the dark recesses of self-pity, with constant questioning of "Why me? Why us? I didn't sign up for this!" For me, it's very easy to go to the "Why Mike?" "Why my marriage of 40 years?" "Why does my family have to deal with this?" It has been said that we go through various trials in life to learn lessons. I found myself calling out to God and the Universe, "Okay, I got it! Whatever I was supposed to learn, I learned it. Just stop the lessons!"

You're going to feel just like this at times. Perhaps you've caught yourself shouting up at the heavens, "It's not fair," "We didn't deserve this!" Perhaps you are putting on a "brave face," while inwardly wondering if you can make it one more day. I often did that – smiling through my sorrow. Many of my friends told me that I was a hero, an angel, a warrior, a role model. *Hah!* This disease has brought me to my knees in despair, killing my spirit over and over. But, just as the phoenix must rise, you cannot let this disease *take two people with it!*

Unfortunately, it is inevitable that dementia will take your loved one, but you must remain strong and not allow it to take you with it. Remember, you must remain strong and not allow this disease to take TWO instead of ONE! There is a saying, "Life is for the living," so you must actively practice living to the fullest, even though you are watching your dearest person slowly, slowly, slowly die right in front of you. As it has been said, "The long goodbye." It is up to YOU to make this time a time of growth, love and survival for you. Is this selfish? No, because your family needs you. Your friends need you. You need you. Your loved one's journey is not yours. Yes, you are the caregiver, but you do not have the actual disease. If you allow your mind to be weak, you can also be the victim of this disease. Here's some points that worked for me and may work for you to keep a positive attitude during this terrible time:

1. Remember that it is nobody's fault that your loved one has this disease. I know it's a popular saying that with "Karma" people get what they deserve. So, did my husband and/or I do something that "earned" us this punishment? I don't believe so, and if you take that as your idea, you will be short-changing yourself from lessons from this part of your journey. Remember, it's not his fault, it's not your fault, it's the disease's fault. Why does this disease exist? That answer will be one to take up with your maker at the right time. Until then, we need to limit the negative impact and the number of victims that the disease will take from this earth.

2. Did you know that a large percentage of caregivers of dementia patients die before the person with dementia? Thirty percent of caregivers die before the people they care for. However, illness that doesn't lead to actual death is rampant and depression and auto-immune diseases are high on the list. For caregivers over the age of 70, the percentage is even higher. 70 percent of all caregivers over the age of 70 die first. So, it's not a joke or something to take lightly to tell yourself to put yourself first. Remember how they say you must put on your own life mask before you can take care of another? Well, in this situation, it's the same thing. You must

make your mental state of mind living with a positive attitude a top priority. I have studied PMA (Positive Mental Attitude) philosophies for decades. If you are new to this concept, please research PMA on the internet, search for caregiver support groups, sign up for daily affirmations, use post-it notes to frame your attitude with sayings such as, "If a man has done his best, what else is there?" George S. Patton, Jr.; "I have learned that success is to be measured not so much by the position that one has reached in life as by the obstacles which one has overcome while trying to succeed." Booker T. Washington; "Whether you think you can or think you can't – you are right." Henry Ford; "Failure to prepare is preparing to fail." Coach John Wooden; "You may have to fight a battle more than once to win it." Margaret Thatcher.

3. Gratitude is the great reality adjuster. Just when you feel your mind start to dwindle down to the lowest levels of "poor me," STOP. Take out a piece of paper or a journal and write down 10 things you are grateful for in your life. Some days, it will be the lowest denominator of things: I can walk; I can see; I have a job; I have one good friend. On other days, your heart will open like floodgates with gratitude for bountiful faith, friends, family, resources. The point is that you should start your day with gratitude. The mind is like a magnet, so when we focus on things we are grateful for, more like-minded things come our way. Oh sure, you say, I tried it once and my life was still filled with all sorts of set-backs, disappointments and conflict. This disease will challenge you in many ways: how many times can you change the adult diaper of your loved one on your way out to an event and the person has an upset stomach; how many times can you look over your bank statement and wonder where will the funds come for all the bills pouring in; how many times can you see your friends happily celebrating anniversaries that you always envisioned you'd be celebrating with your loved one before you are "broken." It has been said that we must be "broken" to become strong. Praise God or Life for the "Good" things in your life and minimalize the "Bad" things in your life. Dig into your heart for the qualities that make us human: compassion, love, forgiveness, empathy. I

have kept a journal focusing on gratitude, memories and goals for many years. I also enjoy looking at "memories" on my Facebook page. They remind me of good times with Mike and my family and although I'm saddened at the progression of the disease, I can hold onto the good memories we did have.

4. Take care of your health. It's easy when you are constantly going to doctors for your loved one to ignore your own health needs. You may think, "What's the point? My little health concerns are nothing compared to his!" It is imperative that you continue with annual visits to your doctor(s) and seek out techniques for rest and relaxation. Your usual visit to the hairdresser, purchase of current fashions, skin care and massage are not luxuries – they are necessities. Male caregivers, no, you're not going to grow that beard because she won't notice anymore! Don't ignore your monthly trip to the barbershop – the comradery is important to your well-being. Don't stuff your feelings with cookies and potato chips! You must feel and look your best if you are to make it on this journey. You must gear up for long term, because it you "let yourself go," this disease will delight in taking two victims with it instead of one. You can only do so much to stop the disease in your loved one (remember, you did not cause it; your loved one did not cause it) but you can do everything to limit the impact of this disease on your life, without depriving your loved one.

Think of it this way: I know Mike loved me and our grown children and grandchildren. Would he want our lives to be ruined forever by something that he cannot control or something he never asked for? No, he would want us to continue to move on with life and live life to the fullest. You are not selfish to take good care of yourself first. You matter too.

REFLECTION
YOUR TURN

1. *Think about your attitude. Do you grumble and complain about your situation? Or, do you try to seek out the positives in your life? Write your thoughts down here:*

_____

_____

_____

_____

_____

_____

2. *Write down 10 things you are grateful for in your life right now. Then, write down 5 more things you are grateful for regarding your loved one's condition. (This will be harder. Think of gifts of the heart, such as compassion, patience, etc.) Write down here:*

_____

_____

_____

_____

_____

_____

Chapter 7

The New "Normal"

$\mathcal{D}$o you like change? Most people don't. We usually feel comfort and security in having things the way they are, the way they've always been, especially if things are going along pretty well. Some of the biggest changes that can cause an internal explosion in a person include the death of a child, the death of a spouse, parent or loved one, diagnosis of an incurable disease, loss of a job, loss of a good friendship or drama/conflict among close relationships. Even things such as retirement, selling a family home, or even a vacation that are supposed to be positives can put a person through the uneasiness of change. As a caregiver of a person with dementia, you need to get to used to change and even embrace each new change as your new "normal." It's the only way you'll survive.

Memories. They can be your friend, or a roadblock to adjustment. For example, when I saw my memories of years past, I saw pictures of my husband in a way better state of health that showed just how much he did deteriorate at the end of his life. "Wow, he was so with it back then. And that was only a year ago, 6 months ago . . ." The mind wants *those* days back, not the way it's now. But, this disease has no cure and the patients only further progress down as per basic functions such as toileting, eating for themselves, and/or expressing ideas in words. Plus, it's a tricky path that deceives a person into thinking the loved one is getting better. Every once in a while, the brain synapses fire properly and you'll be amazed by comments that your loved one says. For example, a good friend was visiting my husband in the assisted living facility and she said that a nurse would be by "sooner or later." My husband quipped to her, "Probably later than sooner." We were pretty shocked that he said this because he had only been speaking "gibberish," and we felt that that statement was more complex because he had to switch the words around, not just repeat something. But it was just an anomaly – he went back to his usual nonsensical language.

When we bring him home on Sundays to have dinner with his children and grandchildren, he has said things such as, "Can I have a beer?" the answer is "No, dad. You're not allowed beer anymore," or he points to a picture on the wall and says, "There's Michelle" (our oldest daughter). These moments are treasured by us as they represent a small breakthrough in our new normal. It's like in the famous Nicholas Sparks novel/movie "The Notebook," when his wife has the recognition that the love story he is telling her about is about "her," but then the tangles of this disease rob her of any continued understanding and she goes back to her lost state. It is a cruel disease indeed.

Here's an example of how you may need to adjust to the new normal as I had to do with pertaining to our driving to places together. My husband used to have an excellent sense of direction and he not only was a good driver, but he also loved to drive. We did many, many road trips in our marriage from Florida to our hometowns in the suburbs of Chicago. We also drove to and from a favorite vacation spot in Tennessee and to and from some acreage we bought in Southern Illinois. Mike was always the driver. After it was necessary for Mike to no longer drive, I did all the driving, but I wasn't comfortable with long road trips, so we no longer drove to our vacations places any more. For a while, we were able to still travel, but we flew and then rented a car, which I drove. So, for a period of time, this was our "new normal." We adjusted, because Mike still had a pretty good sense of direction. Then came the time when I got lost with a car rental and went the wrong way out of the airport. I knew my husband used to know the way to my mom's home, but he couldn't offer me any advice, (and some of the things he told me to do were totally opposite.) This frustrated me to no end; I felt hopeless and helpless. Then, my new normal started to consist of "Mapquest" for everything, along with written directions in my "simple" terms (sense of direction is not my strong suit.) For most cases, this suited our purposes and Mike was still able to get in and out of the car in the passenger seat, no problem. So, this was our "new normal." Then, Mike's disease progressed even further when he no longer knew how to go to the passenger side and open the door (sometimes he'd go in the back seat or wander off to another car.) So now, I had to walk him to the passenger seat, open the door and shut it. Once in, I would have to fasten his seat belt. He no longer could figure out how to do this once simple, automatic task. By the time my daughters and I took him out for our 40th Anniversary dinner, he no longer knew how to get in the car. We had to give him a lift and a push and swing his legs in the car. We had to do a similar procedure to get him out. Also, by this time, he was in adult diapers full-time, so we had a waterproof pad on the car seat (just in case) and also had an "adult diaper bag" filled with diapers, wipes and plastic gloves in case an emergency necessitated a restroom visit. This was the 4th "new normal" in this example. Once Mike was in a wheelchair full time and a resident at the assisted living facility, we no longer drove him in our car. We were fortunate that he was comfortable taking the Connection Bus to travel our house on Sundays because they are equipped with a wheelchair lift that makes his travel possible. So, you can see that as a caregiver to a loved one, you must constantly adjust, change, adapt to deteriorations in your loved one's capabilities.

This example is just one of countless adjustments you will be making in your relationship, including feeding, toileting, sleeping, intimacy, conversing – every aspect of your lives. If you constantly lament the "way it used to be," and "he used to be able to do it this way ..." you will be trapped in misery and unable to move forward in your life in a positive way.

Here's some tips on keeping up with the constantly changing "new normals."

1. Recite the serenity prayer: "God, grant me the serenity to accept the things I cannot change, Courage to change the things I can, and wisdom to know the difference." That about sums it up. There are many things about this disease that we simply have no control of. Accept them and look at the things you can control.

2. Create a metaphor or use imagery in your mind to replicate your life; imagine your life as a journey or a river that flows constantly forward with many twists and turns, but always moving forward.

3. Avoid negative language such as, "I'm done," "I can't take this," or "This is too far. I'm out of here." Sayings like these are like a red stop sign, prohibiting you from moving forward. Remember the saying, "This too shall pass."

4. Practice the 5 P's: Prior Planning Prevents Poor Performance. For example, don't forget to pack that Adult Diaper Bag and don't forget to charge your cell phone so your Maps app works. I've learned to bring the extra battery charger device in my purse so I don't end up with a dead phone.

   In conclusion, I wish I could make it easier for you, but you've probably already noticed that this disease is a series of adjustments in the functionality in your relationship. I encourage you to "go with the flow," with the least resistance and an "I've got this," attitude to stay afloat of this family illness.

REFLECTION
YOUR TURN

Think of one example where you had to adjust to a series of "New Normals" in your caregiving journey. Please write it down here:

_____

_____

_____

_____

_____

_____

_____

Now, create your life's metaphor or imagery for dealing with these constant intrusions in your natural life's flow. Write it here so you can remember it. Use as many sensory details as possible:

_____

_____

_____

_____

_____

_____

_____

Chapter 8

Jealousy and Anger

*J*ealousy and anger – two of the most damaging emotions that will wreak havoc on your successful journey as a caregiver. Plus, they are intertwined with each other: feelings of jealousy can lead to anger. Here's some tips to conquer these two negative forces in your success as a caregiver.

As stated before in Chapter 7, you will most likely encounter a series of setbacks necessitating a "new normal." One example of how jealous feelings can come up is when you see happily-married couples, who are in your circle of friends, enjoying traveling, going on cruises, celebrating double-digit anniversaries, etc. Of course, you love them, and you are happy for them, but then that old yellow-eyed demon, jealousy, pops up with its ugly head, telling you, "Wasn't that supposed to be you and Mike? Weren't you working your whole life to enjoy traveling during the 'Golden Years'?" Then, you're tired and you just helped your loved one shower, get dressed for bed including adult diaper, and sit down for a few moments of solitary peace and he pops up around the corner, out of bed, looking around for God knows what! Cousin "anger" pops up, and you angrily yell, "Get back in bed. I did all that work and you're not going to be up now bothering me anymore. I have a JOB! I'm done with you," and you march him back to bed. If you had a video in my home, you would have seen this occur on occasion, followed by guilty feelings of remorse, "It's not his fault," "He didn't do anything wrong."

The best way to avoid the ugly consequences of anger and guilt is to not let yourself get seduced by jealousy. For me, I had to get used to the idea that when there were things that Mike could no longer go to, I had to go alone. This was a big adjustment for someone who was married for 40 years and who was considered "Mike and Mary." For example, I met up with some childhood friends of Mike's, who also became my friends over the years. At first, I felt like a third wheel, but then I took on the challenge of trying to enjoy the event as an individual and trying to learn something in every activity I went to. At a recent wedding, my sister-in-law, who is a widower, turned to me and said, "This is when it hurts," when the wedding DJ announced, "All the couples on the dance floor," followed by a sweep of adoring couples. Then, "All the couples married for at least 20 years on the dance floor," and some of the couples swept off. And it went on until 50 years, and I couldn't help but feel a ping of loss and possibly envy for the couples still on the dance floor for 40 years, because had Mike been able to attend the wedding, that would have been us. But, realistically, is life ever easy? Is life ever fair? So, you just have to pull your head up, shoulders back, smile and continue. A strategy of "serving others" in this situation can help. For example, I love to take photos, so I took it upon myself to take photos of all of the couples around the table and send them copies. I also posted them to the Facebook post on the wedding and felt happy to see all of the appreciative comments. The quickest way to turn a "pity party" into something mentally healthier is to create a "service act." Giving to others is a way to turn emotions outward toward a desirable effect.

If you feel that you are losing the "jealousy and anger" battle, please seek professional help. Anxiety and depression are by-products of these negative emotions. I personally haven't taken anti-depression pills, but your doctor can advise you if they would help your situation. Be transparent with your professional about your feelings. Sometimes just having someone to talk to can really help.

Just knowing that these are two issues you will have to deal with will help prepare you for situations in which they may occur. Here's some tips:

1. Don't compare yourself with others. No one can be you as well as you.
2. When others gush and brag to you about their fabulous lives, you may want to seek more non-ego driven friends.
3. Look for simple pleasures in life. A few moments of peace. A quiet walk in your garden. A rip-roaring comedy on Netflix. Instead of thinking of all the things you can no longer do with your loved one, think of things you can do.
4. Don't be afraid to go it alone. Have you gone to a movie alone? Well, there's always a first time for everything. Sometimes you just can't find someone to go with, so buy yourself some candy and popcorn and enjoy the newest release in one of those super comfy lounge chairs. I created a "movie club," consisting of similar lady friends of mine, and we go to shows together regularly and have a blast.
5. Keep learning and growing. Take up painting, quilting, home decorating, or crafts. Explore some of the new-age trends: aroma therapy, meditation, yoga, numerology, readings. Read, journal, reflect, speak, teach. Life is here for the living. Don't forget to Live It!

To sum up, don't compare your new perhaps somewhat saddened life to others. Remember, no one can be you as wonderfully as you can. By using these tips, you can ward off the two deadly emotions: jealousy and anger.

REFLECTION
YOUR TURN

1. *Think of a time when you were red-hot jealous of another person or couple. Then, think of when you got angry with the person you are taking care of. Write these slices-of-life here:*

   _____

   _____

   _____

   _____

   _____

   _____

   _____

2. Re-read some of the tips mentioned in this chapter for fighting off "Poor me" attitudes. Now, write down 3 concrete ones that you will put into action today.

   _____

   _____

   _____

   _____

   _____

   _____

Chapter 9

Isolation and Connections

For two years, my husband attended adult day care, every weekday, Monday to Friday. The Connection Bus would pick him up every morning between 7 and 7:30 and bring him home between 4 and 4:30. I was still working as a teacher, trying to fulfill my 5-year DROP retirement program. Luckily, my school principal and administration supported me once I was totally transparent with my situation and they gave me Periods 1 and 2 for planning, so I could be a little later on my arrival time at school (8 a.m. instead of 7:30 a.m.) I had a routine of making his breakfast of a few sausages or bacon, toast, coffee, juice, helping him shower, laying out his clothes, helping him dress, put on his socks and shoes – all before I got ready for my job! Then, there was managing his meds – morning meds after breakfast and having to have the exact change ($3.50) for the bus, each way. Of course, the situation was the same for the return trip. We had electric gates for security, so I had to be home every day to open the gates, get the money ready for the bus (I eventually ordered tickets, but that was still a process). My husband was a friendly man, so he usually was very affectionate toward the drivers who walked him up to the door, shaking their hands, etc. On a few occasions, however, he told wild stories about where they had been, gambling and drinking, going into basements where there were piles of gold (all hallucinations.)

Since he had "Lewy Body Disease" in the mid-stages by this time, I often gave him Melatonin or even a beer to calm his shakes. He was wearing one-pound wristbands to steady his hands, so when he ate, it was always hit or miss what he actually ate, dropped on the floor or missed until trying several times.

Because of the time restraints and additional caregiving chores, personal time for outside leisure or recreation went on the back burner. Invitations for TGIF with fellow teachers, evening exercise or yoga classes and weekend events were most usually declined. The weekends were long. It was a time when I should be resting and getting rejuvenated for my work week; instead my days were filled with not only the usual household chores I had always done such as housecleaning, laundry, bill paying, but also all the other activities he would usually be in charge of – the yard mowing, small household repairs like garbage disposals or leaking pipes, sprinkler system, etc. I had to have an array of "handymen" available at additional costs. Lawn service — $100 a shot; pool — $80 a month; and all sorts of additional household and yard necessities at $15 to $20 an hour for handymen services. I tried to keep cash on hand for these inevitable occurrences, but of course, these extra expenses were a strain on my budget.

I kept up a "date night" with my husband as long as possible on the weekends just so I could have something away from caregiver chores. Usually, it was dinner and a movie, or just a movie. Leaving him alone at these places to run to the restroom was always an issue and I made a special point of going to places that had a "Family" restroom where we could both go in. I wasn't afraid to ask for help when needed. Many a movie theater usher guarded the women's or men's restroom while I rushed him into the handicapped bathroom stall, leading him as quickly as possible, while he strolled along. Often at restaurants, I would have to have a man check on him as he was taking so long; one time I was told he was found washing his hands in the urinal! The turning point of this was when we had to switch to men's adult underwear. It happened after I found him standing in a pile of urine right outside the men's bathroom at a movie theater. Apparently, he didn't make it in time and his shorts and underwear were soaked. I wrapped a sweatshirt around his hips, told a movie attendant that there was an accident, and moved him quickly to our car. I loaded up the seat with any and all towels, jackets, etc. so as to not stain the car seats. I felt so hopeless and let my emotions all out. After this episode, I moved to him wearing adult underwear at all times, which is definitely a whole different dimension of a very difficult situation.

More and more, it just seemed like too much work to keep going out. Hence, feeling more and more isolated and reclusive. We are unique in our neighborhood in that we have a gathering place at a neighbor's driveway, where friends go on Saturdays to sit around and share conversation over a few beers. I'll always be grateful for those nights where Mike was always welcomed with loving arms, and any new decline in his abilities was not questioned. (Thanks Dave Bradshaw and friends!)

Thus, for a caregiver to survive, he or she will need other connections than those with their loved one. As the disease progresses, they will not be able to give you basic human needs that you are accustomed to, namely conversation, discussion, planning, intimacy. When vows are for "Until Death Do Us Part," when your loved one is totally incontinent for both areas and unable to communicate, you may feel like you are being drawn into the dark abyss yourself, especially if you've had a close long-standing relationship. At some point, you may feel like you are the one dying inside – a little bit at a time. At this point, you need to establish a network of connections so this disease doesn't claim "two" instead of "one" victim. Consider the following:

- Taking a day off work to attend a monthly support group. I was able to attend a three-day Lewy Body conference in Fort Lauderdale, where I made valuable connections with other caregivers going through similar experiences.
- Internet support groups. Although I personally didn't use any of these, I did know that they were available if I so desired.

- Facebook or other social media connections. Because I was totally transparent about our situation and my husband's disease, my Facebook friends offered me many hours of compassion, wisdom, and vicariously shared in my grief and problems.

- It's important to not feel like a victim of this situation. It is imperative to maintain good family relationships as I strove to do with my weekly "Sunday Fun Days" with my grown children and grandchildren, a tradition I maintained even when Mike was living in his assisted living facility for dementia patients. We had him get picked up in his wheelchair and brought to the house for these events as often as possible.

- Travel. Because I was a teacher, I was able to go on educational tours with colleagues in my time off, including summers. It always took double time to arrange for care (prior to his going to assisted living) but it was worth it. I had to do a lot of work beforehand, such as finding in-house live-in care for a week or counting on my family to watch him. These respite activities were integral to keeping my spirit alive and never getting up.

REFLECTION
YOUR TURN

1. *What are some ways your life has become more isolated due to your loved one's disease?*

_____
_____
_____
_____
_____
_____

2. *Write down some specific ways you are still building connections with others, despite limitations:*

_____
_____
_____
_____
_____
_____

3. *Brainstorm some additional ways you can continue to find your life's purpose. Remember "Life is for the Living." Breathe deeply and find new purpose in your life, while continuing with your caregiving for your loved one. You must separate in some ways to keep your flame alive.*

_____
_____
_____
_____
_____
_____

Chapter 10

Taboo Topics

*L*oss of intimacy after years of a mutually satisfying relationship. Add into the mixture that one partner is no longer able to be a part of the relationship because the loved one is not mentally capable of stimulating conversation, mental bonding, shared remembrances, and has now been placed in a facility away from home. What does the other healthy partner with all the same sexual and relationship needs do? In some cases, they turn to another person to fill this need. This is a very Taboo Topic that no one will talk about because it is so embodied by guilt.

Through my years of researching caregiver stories and talking to lots and lots of caregivers in confidential settings, I have heard about these taboo topics. I met a man on an airplane, who told me his son and his wife were trying to get him certified as incompetent because he had feelings for his wife's in-home caregiver, a young, pretty woman. When his wife, who had Alzheimer's, died, the man began paying the woman's rent, buying her children toys, clothes and school supplies. The widower was enraged because he told me he felt like his son was treating him as a child and he was fully aware of what he was doing with this woman and his money. He told me he loved her and wanted to take care of her. I asked him if they were intimate (as he was about 80 years old) and he said that they hugged and kissed. He was in love with her. His son filed a complaint with the woman's agency, saying that she was taking advantage of his father in a vulnerable time and the woman was in jeopardy of losing her job. I asked his permission to share his story because I told him I was writing a caregiver book, and he said, "Sure." He was very sad because he said that his son's relationship with him had soured upon his wife's death. He shared that he gave his daughter-in-law a real mink coat that had been his wife's coat to keep it in the family. The last time he visited his son's home, he asked to see the coat and he was told that they sold it. He was devastated. He felt betrayed and this incident, combined with how his son was treating him with his "affair" with this young woman, was leading him to consider writing his son out of his life and will!

Another male caregiver had cared for his wife for years in the home, over 8 years. Upon her passing, he immediately married another woman and his friends supported his decision, commending him on his years of caregiving to his wife. Apparently, he had had a long-standing relationship with this woman on the side and only made it "legal" upon his wife's death.

In our society, people love to "judge" others and their behaviors. I've always thought that people judge others to make themselves feel better about their own situation, whatever it is. If the other person has it "bad," then their life must be better and good! Without naming names, one husband of over 50 years of marriage to his beloved wife who had an 8-year bout with Alzheimer's, had a secret "girlfriend" with whom he visited restaurants, drinking establishments and even met up with her in his and her separate homes. This woman showed up at his funeral. Everyone knew that it was his girlfriend. Whispers and gossip were an undercurrent at his funeral, which was a year after his wife's passing.

Here's some ideas to ponder: Make your health — mental, emotional — a top priority. Do not rush into the arms of a total stranger who may bring you that something to fill the void in your life, but also bring you an unexpected diagnosis of STD, HIV, separation with your children, or loss of your bank account savings!

If you feel you must fill the void of intimacy for your own emotional health, consider some of the following:

- Seek out the companionship of a mutual person who knows and understands your situation. Sometimes a conversation with an understanding member of the opposite sex will satisfy your need for compassion and intimacy.

- Make sure the person has your best intentions at heart and not ulterior motives of getting your money or other possessions. Many a man has been lured by a flirtatious complimentary woman and many a woman has been swindled by the charming adoring words of a gentleman who makes her feel like a princess.

- Beware of online scammers. Being in a vulnerable position sends out distress signals, but also signals of opportunities of sexual and financial conquest, to unscrupulous scammers.

- If you decide that you do want to engage in a full intimate relationship with another person other than your loved one, think deeply about the consequences upon your relationships with your friends, your children, your co-workers, and your friends at your place of worship. Will they judge you? Will they end their relationship with you? Is it worth the price? Guard your heart above all else and remember that you are in a vulnerable position.

So, in conclusion, there are many Taboo Topics when it comes to the caregiver's life. Trust your judgment, seek advice, seek connections with others to stay part of this world. Someone once told me, "Life is for the Living." Continue your path toward living to the best of your abilities.

REFLECTION
YOUR TURN

1. *Be honest with yourself: is there something "taboo" that you are engaging in as a response to the situation in which you find yourself? Consider your thoughts, feelings and actions that may not coincide with your marital vows of "Til death do us part."*

_____

_____

_____

_____

_____

_____

_____

2. *Write down advice to your best friend if he or she was in your position and then take that advice for yourself. Be a bit forgiving of yourself.*

_____

_____

_____

_____

_____

_____

_____

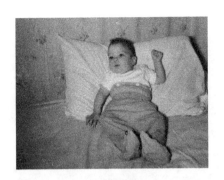

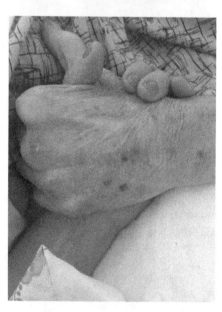

EPILOGUE – The Final Goodbye

I wrote the following sitting next to my husband while he was in his final days of hospice:

I'm bedside next to my husband, who is in what the Hospice doctor calls "A self-induced coma." It marks the third day of no food or water for Mike, with Hospice nurses around the clock, making him comfortable.

Mike fought a valiant battle and his body shows his battle scars. He is around 80 to 90 pounds. He was a big guy, 265 pounds at his highest. His body has at least five wound bandages that the nurses change daily, marking the bandage change date with a permanent marker. They are called "terminal wounds" because they will never heal because the body cannot heal itself any longer and medicine can only do so much. He's sleeping comfortably now, with minimal amounts of morphine to help him feel comfortable. His thin body is covered with a blanket that covers his body frame with legs in permanent L-shapes from the rigidity of his disease. His once robust face is now drawn, with a steady stream of breath from his open mouth: breathe in, breathe out.

As I sat there bedside, holding my husband's hand, I overhead an obviously frazzled wife a few years younger than my age with her husband going through his chest of drawers in the bed area in our same joint room. Her husband is a big guy, like my husband used to be, and still "ambulatory," meaning still able to walk. He was following her saying over and over again, "Let's go. Let's go." "Where did all your socks go?" she muttered, out loud. "You had six pairs of socks here just last week." It was as if I was looking at myself and my husband in years past, which seemed like a long, long journey ago.

I said in a caring voice, "They misplace clothes here all the time. You're supposed to write their name on them and they should do small laundry batches to keep them together, but I don't think they do, because he's often in someone else's clothes."

She welcomed my comments and we looked at each other, recognizing the situations with our husbands that we both shared, at different time periods of the progression of the disease. I recognized her for the warrior she was, as I felt she looked at me the same way. I learned she had just admitted her husband to the empty bed in my husband's room. Over the next 25 minutes, we exchanged commonalities that we both had been through — I, close to the end of my caregiving journey, and she, marking five years of a situation, "That I wouldn't wish on my worst enemy," as she put it. Mike had an amazing Hospice nurse, nicknamed "Miracle," and he and I both fist-bumped her, marking her five years as a caregiver.

She told me her story: her husband got his dementia early, at age 60, and she decided she had to put him in a facility when she reached her "last straw." It happened when she was cooking dinner and her back was to her husband. He was anxious about something and pushed her up against the cabinet. She was only about 120 pounds so she said her face got cut and started to bleed. She was so stunned she didn't even cry. Her husband had never been violent to her. She had said that it was her "final straw" with many straws I recognized, including:

- Nonsensical communication where he would repeat the same things over and over until she was totally stressed.
- Wanting to go "home" when he was already home. I told her a tip another caregiver had told me about how we put Mike in his car, drove around the block and then came home, announcing, "You're home. You're home." Then he would be fine. It worked.
- She said she was still stressed after placing him in the home and her friends told her it's separation anxiety and she said no she's perfectly fine on her own. It's all the paperwork for Medicaid and nursing homes, frustration and feeling that she is still young, 64, and this is a life she wouldn't wish on anyone.

Perhaps you can relate; I know I did. I told her maybe God selected us as special people to be caregivers to our loved ones. I told her my journey was almost over but hers still had a way to go and to call me if she had any questions. It's for people like Rene that I wrote this book.

Rene, you are a true warrior; you are not alone.

#

Mike passed after a little longer than a week in his "self-induced" coma. It was on a Sunday morning, so instead of going to church, I sat by his side, held his hand, and repeated the St. Jude prayer and other devotionals out loud. I thanked him for being a great husband and father to our children. I thanked him for understanding me like no one else could. And then he simply passed away. There was no loud breath as I expected, but he just slipped off after a long, long battle. I am so thankful that I was able to be there when he passed to the other world beyond.

I'm sharing with you a copy of a few of the memory pieces we read at Mike's Celebration of Life.

To conclude, life is an ongoing event, and when you feel all alone and like no one understands what you're going through, I hope my experience can be of value to you with encouragement and hope for the future. You are special and of great worth. Thank you for being a caregiver to your loved one. It is important work. You are important. Never forget that.

My Memories of Mike Monroe (read at his Celebration of Life)

I was a young girl of 23 and he was 26 when we met through a mutual friend at a weekend-long celebration of our Country's 200th Birthday, July 4, 1976 in Carbondale, Illinois. I wore a white bikini and cut-offs most of that weekend, but Mike was pre-occupied with his 13 new puppies by his dog and constant companion at that time, Tonja. I thought to myself, "Well, he's very paternal. That's a good sign for being a father." He asked for my phone number and said he would call me when he moved back to Chicago, as he had just graduated with a double major he was so proud in, Agriculture and Business.

I figured I'd never hear from him again, but he did call, and our first date was at Salerno's Pizza in Berwyn. It didn't take us too long to fall in love and start planning a lifetime together – just a few months. We married the following Oct. 22, 1977 and it was 40 years this past Oct.

After the Chicago blizzard of '79 in Chicago, Il., we moved to Florida, where we raised four children in Lake Worth. Our lives were filled with love, hopes for the future and family and friends. Our home was in the Biltmore acres area, so our children grew up in a country-like setting and we had an array of animals on our acre and a half: a horse, ponies, chickens, sheep, goats, turkeys, pigs and rabbits.

Mike loved the outdoors. You'd always see him outdoors in his blue jean shorts, work boots, safety goggles and ball cap working on his plants or building cages for the many animals on our homestead.

Mike loved to drive, and we drove back to Chicago many Christmas and every summer to see his family, including his parents, sisters and brothers and their families. We'd usually stay at my mom's home and visit my side of the family, we always ate at Shoney's, and he would chant, "Shoney's, Shoney's." Buffets were his thing with four children to feed!

We were very fortunate that Mike had a close group of friends in Chicago, who he grew up with who became my friends too. And then we enjoyed our friends here in Florida. We brought in the New Year almost on an annual basis and the memories will never fade.

Mike loved beer as you all know. It wasn't unusual to see him with a cooler in his arm filled with cold beer and Mike was good with money. He was a stock investor, coin collector, stamp collector, golf club collector. He was frugal but generous also, and he loved gambling, the Derby, playing the ponies and investing in properties, in which he made enough money to provide security for me and his family.

His favorite sports event of all time was the Kentucky Derby and he loved golf.

But most of all, Mike loved our children and me. I never doubted that for a minute. Our firstborn Michelle and he had a special bond. She was like him in many ways, and he brought her on trips to Chicago and built her horse stall for her champion horse that she won many ribbons with, King Shy Dancer. First born son Mark was named after his brother Mark, whom he was very close to. He never missed one of Mark's Basketball games. He was so happy to have a son to continue the Monroe name.

His third child Marcie was a chip off the old block. She shared his friendly disposition and was a great baseball player, like her dad. Like her siblings, Marcie helped a lot with Mike during his sickness. Marcie also is a bit of a hippy, like her dad!

Fourth child Melody was his Bonus Baby, making him a father again at age 44. Melody inherited Mike's saving of money characteristic from him, plus his innate sense of driving and directions. She just drove me to Chicago this past summer. She also got her independent free spirit from her dad and they also shared a strong bond.

Mike loved his three grandchildren and cared for his children's loves.

And he loved me, his wife. I always knew that and felt that in my deepest parts of my soul. He was my godsent mate and beloved husband for 40 years. He was an easy-going husband, never had a bad word to say about anyone and never failed to tell me that he loved me, I "looked good" and that the meal I cooked was the best he ever had.

I loved Mike with my whole heart and loved and cherished the life we built together, our happy home with cherished children and friends.

He fought a valiant battle for six years with Lewy Body Dementia, and Alzheimer's, with no cure. The cruelest of diseases that robs people of their memories and Golden Years.

He will always be remembered for all the quirky things he did like:

1. Always going to buffets like Shoney's or Golden Corral.
2. Driving his golf cart around the neighborhood, but if the kids wanted to, he said it was broken.
3. Cooking up mystery pots of stew or soup with leftovers from the refrigerator.
4. Collecting all sorts of odds and ends from golf clubs to matches to sports memorabilia.
5. Watching TV sports from women's tennis to golf.

I imagine him now being welcomed into heaven by loved ones, and he, with his big robust voice, saying, "I'm here! Whoo hooo!" I know he would tell each and every one of you here that he loved and cared about you and he appreciated everything you did for him, especially during his illness, like when Debbie made him his Mike ball hat and birthday cake for his birthday, when all of you accepted him through the various stages of his disease, through the tremors, the falls, the hospital visits, and the constant prayers for me also and his family.

All I know for sure is I am sure happy I was fortunate to meet Gopher, which was his nickname, on July 4, 1976, and I thank him for being my husband and the father of four children and a best friend and lover to me. I sure wish his life didn't end this soon, but none of us know God's plans. Just like Impressionist art, if you look closely, you just see dots, but if you look away, you see the big picture and why something was supposed to be the way it was.

So, to Michael S. Monroe, thank you for giving me a great life. Thank you for being a great provider so I have a home to live in. I love you and always will. Your wife, Mary

Michael S. Monroe (aka Gopher)

*H*ello, my name is Bill Phillips, born in Chicago, grew up in Westmont, IL. Although the good Lord blessed me with four great sisters, he never gave me a brother. Mike, you were that brother; my brother, from another mother.

We were a school year apart but had a brotherly bond from the beginning. We attended the same Catholic Grade School, Holy Trinity. We attended the same Catholic High School, St. Procopius Academy but graduated from public school, Hinsdale Central. The reasoning, our parents were old school, we were paying our own high school tuition, later on, we wanted that money for ourselves... We both attended College of DuPage after high school, interrupted by military service, back to C.O.D. and then on to SIU - Carbondale where we graduated from in 1976 and 1977 respectfully.

Mike and I were altar boys, often served Mass together. We were on the same Little League Team, the Barbers and 1962 Champions. Was he ever upset when he wasn't in the Championship Team picture because of a family vacation!

We then caddied at Hinsdale Golf and Country Club. Maintaining our Catholic upbringing, we attended the early Mass on Sundays. It was either 6:00 or 6:30am. During the heat of summer we always wore shorts. One Sunday, we were asked to leave because of our attire. My mother called the Pastor sticking up for the two of us; she gave him a good lecturing...

My mom was like a second mother to Mike and they had a mutual mother-son love for each other. I'd like to share some of this side of Mike. My mother spent the last four years of her life crippled and in a wheelchair. She had the gift of painting passed on from her father, mostly flowers and landscape. Mike's first job out of college was with Tropical Tree Plants and Rentals or something like that working as a grower in the greenhouses on the northwest side of Chicago. He felt bad for my mother, just like family. When working weekends, he always stopped by the Phillips' home, bringing her both live plants and cut flowers. The living room, dining room and kitchen were always full. Mike said he loved seeing the smile that it brought to her face.

A commonality was our love of German Shepherd dogs and road trips. A great moment in our lives was the road trip to Colorado and Arizona in Mike's old Pontiac Station Wagon. It was the two of us and Mike's dog, Tonya. We left Carbondale after spring finals. It was 90+ degrees out. We hit St. Louis during rush hour. We hit Kansas City when the Royals game was letting out and hit the Colorado border in a blizzard! We couldn't believe it! We visited friends in the Durango area then headed for Tucson, AZ. Broke down in the desert, on an Indian Reservation pushing the car for miles. But, we had fun just experiencing life…

Then there's the pick-up baseball games, the football in the streets and hockey in the Monroe backyard and the many ponds and lakes in the immediate area.

My dad built a swing set in the backyard. Mike and I thought the height was perfect for a goal post so we improvised and added a post on either end and started kicking field goals over it.

Hockey was one of our favorite winter activities. Everyone rotated playing goalie. My turn came and I made a fantastic save on of all people, Charlie. Charlie preceded to pick-up the puck and wings it blind-siding me, fracturing my left cheek bone and orbital eye socket, knocking me unconscious. Mike ran to my parents' house to get my mom or dad telling Charlie, "You are dead meat." Everyone had the fear of Mr. Phillips except for Mike. They had a deep respect for each other.

We were in the same Biology class. Not long after my injury, we had a biology exam. The priest wanted me to remove the eye patch thinking I'd have exam answers inside. Mike blasted the priest telling him "How can he see? It's too close to his face and his eye is swollen shut."

Through the years there were bonfires, picnics, concerts, Loyola Beach keggers, McDowell Woods, Kentucky Derby, Western Open golf tourneys, poker games, golf and our annual Arlington Race Park trips the Saturday before Memorial Day. We had so much fun.

Golf! There are so many golf stories. One stands out. We always enjoyed playing new courses, especially the year they opened like Rend Lake off of I-57 in Benton, IL. Mike could display some temper tantrums on the course. He got so mad at his putting; he threw his putter up in the air. It never came down! It stayed up in a tree... There were the water moccasins at Orchard Lake and the heat at Herrin, ahh, southern Illinois golf!

There are so many good times, so many stories. I promised I'd keep this to two pages because I know Mary and others will have so much to say....

So my best bud, I sure hope you're now horseback riding with daughter Michelle, playing some golf with Charlie, throwing snowballs with Jimmy and bringing flowers to my mom! And last of all, beers and poker, save a seat for me!

Never say good-bye, only see ya... Until we see each other again, although hoping not too soon, I love you brother...

Billy

Valuable Resources You Can Trust

Lewy Body Dementia Association
www.lbda.org
Caregiver toll-free number: 888-204-3054

Alzheimer's Association
www.alz.org
24/7 Helpline: 800-272-3900

Family Caregiver Alliance
www.caregiver.org
Toll-free: 800-445-8106

AARP
AARP.ORG/PREPARE TO CARE
AARP.ORG/CAREGIVING
Toll-free: 877-333-5885

*M*ary A. Monroe has been a published author since 2005, with her celebrated series of books for teens, including *Miracle at Monty Middle School (Spanish version Milagro en la Escuela Monty), Krazy White Girl, Tagger,* and *Tagger Theater/Screenplay version.* She also wrote her mother's biography/narrative, *Henrietta, The Story of My Life.* When her husband was just beginning to realize his disease, he told her, "You're going to write a book about me," and she did. After wondering how she ever would survive supporting her husband through his devastating diagnosis of Lewy Body Dementia and Alzheimer's, she now shares her personal story and lessons-learned for other caregivers in need of hope and encouragement. A devoted mother, grandmother and Language Arts teacher for 22 years, Monroe lives in Lake Worth, Florida. She has her Masters in reading, is Palm Beach County's Teacher of the Year for 2012, and is an event speaker.

marymonroebooks.com